God Speaks...

30 Days of Positioning Yourself to Hear God's Voice

Tameaka Reid Sims

Dedication~

To my parents, Rev. Wesley I. Reid & Kathleen M. Reid for loving me through every decision I have made whether you agreed or not. Thank you for praying for me when I didn't have the wisdom, courage or strength to pray for myself. I thank God that I am your little girl.

~

To Reiley, Joshua, Micah, Jeremiah, & Christopher, a mother's love is unchanging and constant. I will forever move heaven and earth for you. Thank you for sharing in a ministry that you were born into.

~

To my husband Micah C.T. Sims, your love sustains me through the best and the worst of times. Thank you for the freedom you allowed me to throw myself into the pages of this book and for encouraging me to finish.

~

Table of Contents

INTRODUCTION

God Speaks, 30 Days of Positioning Yourself to Hear God's Voice was written out of desperation to identify and clearly hear the voice of God. I needed like never before to connect differently with God. My mind was cluttered, my spirit needed cleansing and I knew it was only through an encounter with God that my situation would change. I was tired of prayer as usual, so I humbled myself, realized my limitations and shortcomings and purposefully made time for God. I began a journey expecting real results from a real God.

I have since come to learn that the process of coming to know God is a rigorous, yet rewarding one that requires diligence, sacrifice and a readiness to evaluate your reality, regardless of what it appears to be in the moment. However, it is most certainly always worth the effort. I believe wholeheartedly that this book will forever change the life of the reader who is willing to go the distance and engage in this transformative spiritual 30 day journey; for it is impossible to seek God, experience Him and not yearn for more.

Over 21 years of ministry, has taught me many things; one of which is, there is no right or wrong way to pray. In fact, God is always delighted whenever His children choose to talk with Him or simply sit for a while in His presence. 1 Thessalonians 5:17 tells us that we must pray without ceasing, which suggests that prayer is not only a form of communication between God and the believer, but it is intended to be adopted as a lifestyle. There are so many benefits to having a healthy, consistent prayer life, most importantly your prayer life determines the depth in which you relate to and experience the movement of God.

I assume that because you have purchased this resource, you are serious about implementing necessary spiritual changes that will ultimately contribute to a rewarding lifestyle of prayer. And I am honored to assist in this exciting process.

Anticipate your 30 day journey to uncover many things about yourself and your relationship with God. I know first hand, because I have walked the road you are preparing to travel. I encourage you to create a devotional space that will serve as your chamber of transformation for the next series of days.

Get your bible, a notebook, a highlighter and a pen so that you have everything you need readily available. It is imperative that you designate time to meditate on your daily scripture readings, internalize each daily prayer and complete each daily assignment.

Utilize the journal pages included in this book; they will help you in days to come as you gauge your progress. Each step is a necessary part of this process and none should be overlooked.

On my 30 day journey, I rested every Sunday, consequently the journey technically takes 34 days from beginning to end. I encourage you to do the same, although it is not required. Taking a Sabbath will allow you to be contemplative about the week behind you, what you learned and how God chose to speak. It will also allow you to be intentional about the week ahead, as you set goals for yourself through this awakening experience.

On this Journey, be steadfast, pay close attention to any whispers and signs along the way, but most importantly, enjoy and finish the journey! I guarantee if you so desire, you will NEVER be the same, because those who seek Him will indeed find Him in wonderful and unexpected ways.

Feb 17, 2022

DAY One ~ Repent

❖ **Repent ye therefore, and be converted, that your sins may be blotted out, when the times of refreshing shall come from the presence of the Lord. Acts 3:19**

Dear Lord,

You are so amazing! No one but YOU can take nothing and create something beautiful, full of potential and promise. I recognize that I am absolutely nothing without You, worthless because I was born in sin. I pray that You will receive me with abundant mercy as I repent of every sinful thought, word and deed committed against You. I realize that in numerous ways I have let You down, therefore I come before You with a repentant heart determined to live a new life. I sincerely ask for forgiveness and an opportunity to start anew.

Lord, I need a refreshing of Your Holy Spirit to make me over. Strengthen me to stand firm in times of doubt, temptation and fear, as You deliver me from being bound by what is comfortable and familiar. I sincerely want you to take control of my heart, mind, spirit, and mouth, in this very moment as I turn from life as usual and yield to Your perfect will for my life. I desire to walk boldly and confidently from now on because today YOU are my choice!

Thank You for loving me enough to see value in such an imperfect person and never losing faith in me. I freely receive You as my redeemer and embrace the undeserved mercy that liberates me to grow in grace and favor. AMEN

TODAY'S ASSIGNMENT: Acknowledge your sin before The Lord. Be honest with God about private temptation and strongholds, accepting the FACT that God possesses the power to make all things new. Write in your OWN words a statement of intention as you move forward from this day letting go of guilt and shame. Begin walking in victory TODAY!!

I intend to wake-up each day with God in mind, knowing that it is by His Grace & appointment that I am still in this body on earth. I was created to do something for the kingdom of God to help prepare the earth for when He comes to dwell with when time comes to an end.

Walking in victory means that I am keeping God at the forefront of my mind knowing that nothing happens in this earth without his knowledge and authority. Because God is always good, everything results in good.

Thoughts of today's journey....

_____

_____

_____

_____

_____

_____

_____

_____

_____

_____

Feb 18, 2022

DAY Two ~ Submit

❖ **In the day when I cried thou answeredst me, and strengthenedst me with strength in my soul. Psalm 138: 3**

Dear Lord,

I confess that I fail to give our relationship the time and attention it deserves. Please forgive me for allowing my personal agenda to take precedence most of the time. I realize I have neglected what should be most important, therefore I am completely submitting today. I will make conscious decisions in adopting necessary lifestyle changes that usher me into a mindset of recommitment.

I recognize that life is chaotic and senseless, when You are not my central focus. Therefore, as of this moment, I refuse to continue living this way. I desire earnestly to be free from patterns and behavior that hinder my blessings and interfere with my purpose. Lord, I long to know You in a new and refreshing way and I am now resolving to run after You relentlessly, until my change comes.

I pray for such an incredible intimate fellowship with You that it becomes impossible to return to my former self. I willfully turn over all of who I am, as You minister to my brokenness and inadequacy throughout this journey. I vow to actively listen and yield to Your voice. AMEN

TODAY'S ASSIGNMENT: Write a personal declaration confessing the desire for a deeper relationship with God and then demonstrate your intentions by committing to the remainder of this 30 day life changing process.

Father in Heaven,

In the Bible, you often say "Know that I am God" That is my desire "to know" and to live as I know that I have a Father in Heaven who is also the Creator of Heaven & Earth and He is always with me waiting for me to talk to Him. A Father that created me to be with Him 4ever, so as I walk & talk I will keep that knowledge in the forefront of my mind. Knowing that I am a part of fixing the world and I can only do that by staying in agreement with you in all things,

Feb 22, 2022

DAY Three ~ Awareness

❖ **What is man, that thou art mindful of him? and the son of man, that thou visitest him? Psalm 8:4**

Dear Lord,

It blesses me so to know that You, the great and mighty Creator, are forever by my side. I delight in Your boundless compassion and I thank You for the peace in knowing that regardless of where I am, I'm never beyond Your reach. I rejoice in the daily evidence of Your presence that convinces me of how I am forever on Your mind. I marvel at how You intentionally take time to show just how significant I am to You; especially when I consider my countless flaws.

I pray Lord that You will continue to develop my sensitivity toward Your presence, that I might not miss Your movement and discern Your voice as You speak.

My heart overflows, as I celebrate You Lord for loving me, longing to be near me and imparting Your spirit within me. AMEN

TODAY'S ASSIGNMENT: Recall the last time you spent uninterrupted time with God. What do you remember most? Spend a few moments journaling about your experience.

About a month ago, I had 2 consecutive days in which I did nothing but read, study & write your word. From morning to late in the evening. IT was a relaxing and peaceful and the more I read, listened to & wrote the more open my eyes became on just how off the mark I have been on who God is and His true relationship with mankind.

I dove into teachings about the Kingdom of God and understood for the 1st time what Jesus was doing during His ministry on earth and what He is doing for us in Heaven everyday. I see now how important my individual role is for the Kingdom & how mankind as a collective fit into the Creator's plan to dwell on earth with us forever. He didn't create robots, He created human beings with a choice to love him s Creator and 15 Heavenly Father!

Thoughts of today's journey....

Spent a lot of time on Youtube "Catching up" on other people stuff. Spent some time on inspirational messages and in thought about where I am in relationship to my purpose for being here. Need to discover the "vessel" God has made available to me gift so I can throw the essence of me into it. I believe many are waiting for me to work that gift so they can discover theirs and help move the world in God's direction. Less time on other people stuff & dedicated time on figuring out my own stuff

Feb 23, 2022

DAY Four ~ Believe

❖ **But as it is written, Eye hath not seen, nor ear heard, neither have entered into the heart of man, the things which God hath prepared for them that love Him.**
1 Corinthians 2: 9-10

If you Love me, obey my commandment

Dear Lord,

Trusting You is often challenging, but my heart's desire is to believe Your word. Uphold me Lord in times of weakness and deliver me from my crippling unbelief that interrupts progress in our relationship. Only with Your guidance Lord, will I stay on course moving toward the future that has been preordained.

← purpose

obedient relationship — compassionate

I want to grow! I want to mature in my faith and confidence in You! I want to continue evolving and become more like Your son Jesus every day. Teach me Lord to stand solely on Your promises, regardless of my eyes may see in a fleeting moment.

write your Word on my heart

Please Lord, teach me to believe Your word as it takes root. I believe You have good things in store for me and that the best is yet to come. Lord, *YOU PROMISED* no good thing would be withheld from me. Therefore I will wait patiently, while You edify me and perform in me Your perfect work.

my destiny was established before I was born.

I need you to help guide me to that destiny.

learn your voice and allow your word to guide my steps down the paths I must go

17

I am convinced that with Your help I will have the victory over unbelief and never again question Your word.

In the name of Jesus I pray. AMEN

TODAY'S ASSIGNMENT: Worship the Lord today with a new song. Free yourself to create meaningful lyrics. Sing your prayers and praise!

Thoughts of today's journey….

The more I understand who God is regarding His relationship with mankind, I feel more & more special, special. I also have a inner desire to please Him, not because He is making me, but because it is blowing my mind that He did all of this so I can be with Him always in a perfect world.

So as I go through my day, I smile more and am more sensitive to the Holy Spirit when I am about to do or say, think or do something that will result in negative energy in the world.

Feb 24, 2022

DAY Five ~ Instruction

❖ Shew me thy ways, O Lord; teach me thy paths,
Lead me in thy truth, and teach me: for thou art
the God of my salvation; on thee do I wait all the
day. Psalm 25:4

Dear Lord,

I praise You for allowing me to share in a
connection that charts the course of my
destiny. I stand in amazement that You love me
enough to chart my path long before I took my
first breath.

I long to be kept in tune with Your word and
plan for my life. Sanctify me to grow continually
in faith, character, and love. As I strive to
develop into your perfect likeness, bless me
with an abundant grace to do so. Teach me
Lord, to walk in a humble, forgiving and
compassionate spirit, that draws others to You.

Please guide me in your truth, overshadowing
any personal agenda that may arise. Deliver me
from the natural inclination to question You and
train my mind to cheerfully obey. Order my
footsteps and immediately redirect me with
Your strong arm, should I lose my way.

I praise You in advance and thank You for detailed instruction that positions me for success in every area of my life. AMEN

TODAY'S ASSIGNMENT: Ask God for clarity regarding your daily assignments. Listen intently, with an open mind and spirit. Record the details of your experience.

Thoughts of today's journey….

_____

_____

_____

_____

_____

_____

_____

_____

_____

_____

_____

_____

DAY Six ~ Capacity

❖ I thank my God always on your behalf, for the grace of God which is given you by Jesus Christ; That in everything ye are enriched by him, in all utterance, and in all knowledge; Even as the testimony of Christ was confirmed in you: So that ye come behind in no gift. 1Corinthians 1: 5

Dear Lord,

Today, I ask for increased capacity for You. Flood my mind and spirit with new knowledge and revelation of who You are. Show me all that you desire me to know and bridge any divide between us.

Prepare me to receive and operate in every good and perfect spiritual gift. Sharpen my discernment and direct me toward ministry opportunities uniquely designed to shape and strengthen my spiritual and natural ability. I pray that I am used to my fullest capacity, completely for Your glory and honor. Keep my mind intact, my spirit sensitive and my heart patterned after Yours.

I welcome an overflow of Your anointing, as I await new experiences that will stretch me and reshape my spirituality. Lord, I long for more of You. Have Your way and fill me, until I can stand no more. AMEN

TODAY'S ASSIGNMENT: Meditate throughout the day, then write the desires of your heart. Record the ministry/spiritual goals you wish to accomplish.

Thoughts of today's journey….

_____

_____

_____

_____

_____

_____

_____

_____

_____

_____

_____

DAY Seven ~ Control

Dear Lord,

You are an awesome and mighty wonder, far beyond my ability to rationalize or comprehend. I am confident that there is none greater than You.

I love You, for in every phase of life You have been with me and NOTHING I'm facing is beyond Your control. As I think of where I've been and where I am being led, I feel an assurance and a peace that is difficult to explain. Repeatedly, You have protected, sustained and directed me. It simply makes sense to trust You with my life.

Bless me Lord with open spiritual eyes, that I may recognize You at work in both comfortable and uncomfortable seasons. Allow the truth to resonate in my spirit that everything I endure is working for my good. Please Lord, speak to my spirit daily, silence any anxiety and grant me boldness to face every mountain with an abundance of unshakable faith.

I bless You for the assurance of knowing You are more than capable to handle my concerns and navigate me though this every season of life. I yield, willingly and completely. AMEN

TODAY'S ASSIGNMENT: Take your time and list 50 attributes of God.

Thoughts of today's journey....

_____

_____

_____

_____

_____

_____

_____

_____

_____

_____

_____

DAY Eight ~ Joy

❖ **For God giveth to a man that is good in his sight wisdom, and knowledge, and joy. Ecclesiastes 2:26**

Dear Lord,

I praise you for the precious joy that is obtainable, when I seek You. Communing with You affects me in such a way that sadness and depression is instantly transformed. I am overcome with thanksgiving to know that unspeakable joy is mine for the asking!

I pray that you will continue to encourage me and increase my passion toward You. Grant me an outlook that is positive and unfazed by insignificant matters. I pray for unrelenting excitement, as I begin to walk into the glorious future reserved for me.

I especially thank You for fierce divine protection, when issues arise that attempt to compromise my security and steal my joy. Words seem inadequate when expressing my gratitude for the seeds of joy that have been planted in the fibers of my being.

Please Lord, speak clearly to me on days when I am tired and feeling uneasy and remind me that YOUR joy IS my constant strength. AMEN

TODAY'S ASSIGNMENT: 1. Write your own Psalm today, praising, exalting, and celebrating God. 2. Display it where you will see it and be encouraged by it (screen saver, nightstand, desk, etc.) 2. Share this Psalm with someone who is losing his or her joy and strength.

Thoughts of today's journey....

_____

_____

_____

_____

_____

_____

_____

_____

_____

_____

_____

DAY Nine ~ Truth

❖ **Every word of God is pure: He is a shield unto them that put their trust in him. Proverbs 30: 5**

Dear Lord,

I praise You because undeniably, You are The Truth. I acknowledge Your word as binding and reliable, yesterday, today and forever. I believe and stand fully persuaded that You are the Great I AM, my Redeemer, my Lord and King!

I am in awe that You are unafraid of my personal truth. It amazes me that I can come before you without judgment or condemnation and leave whole. Thank You Lord for the liberty that you give me in truth.

I declare Your word to be true in my life. I am healed. I am delivered. I am free. You established that these blessings rightfully belong to me, if I trust in Your word and do not doubt. I am confident that Your word is uncompromising and does not fail. I accept Your truth, allowing it eminent domain over my life.

Your word declares I am Yours and it speaks life into my spirit. I am rendered speechless, as I think of how You consider me worthy to walk transparently in Your presence.

I do not have to hide or be ashamed, for Your mercy and compassion covers, forgives me and restores me. How do I adequately say thank You, Lord? AMEN

TODAY'S ASSIGNMENT: Write a letter to God being brutally honest with Him about where you are and how you feel. Demonstrate your faith by surrendering your emotions, joys, disappointments, expectations and fear. Then, await a response.

Thoughts of today's journey....

_____

_____

_____

_____

_____

_____

_____

_____

_____

_____

_____

DAY Ten ~ Chosen

❖ **This is the covenant that I will make with them after those days, saith the Lord, I will put my laws into their hearts, and in their minds will I write them. Hebrews 10: 16**

Dear Lord,

Your works are beyond comprehension and I marvel at how You have intentionally chosen me! You have stopped short of nothing to cultivate our relationship. How do I explain being a priority of the Most High God? I am aware that there is nothing I could do to deserve such an honor and yet I stand daily in wonderment of such undeserved favor.

With all Your might, You love me. With every passing day, I see clear evidence that You are constantly mindful of me. There is no greater reward than knowing I am SPECIAL, and I MATTER to You!

Being chosen by You and loved by You makes my heart sing and my spirit dance. I bow before You in humble adoration, because You didn't have to choose me, yet you did. AMEN

TODAY'S ASSIGNMENT: Establish a devotional routine and transfer it to your daily calendar. Set alarms, if necessary. Prepare yourself to sit still in God's presence without distraction, EVERY DAY. Inform those who will be impacted that this time is officially belongs to God.

Thoughts of today's journey....

_____

_____

_____

_____

_____

_____

_____

_____

_____

_____

DAY Eleven ~ Boldness

❖ According to the eternal purpose which He purposed in Christ Jesus our Lord: In whom we have boldness and access with confidence by the faith of him.   Ephesians 3:12

Dear Lord,

You are above all and deserving of endless praise. Who is like You? What can compare to Your works? I thank You for the blessing of being your child and having unlimited access to You.

I pray that You would grant me the necessary boldness to go, wherever I am sent. Grant me the conviction and fearlessness I need to share enthusiastically the gift of Your saving power. Point out those whose salvation is linked to my witness. Lord, please give me an obedient spirit and remove any self-righteousness that may attempt to surface.

Use me daily to win souls and increase your Kingdom. Use me, Father, to teach others about your son Jesus and lead the lost to eternal life. You have my permission to take my life and use it to Your GLORY!

I humbly render this petition. AMEN

TODAY'S ASSIGNMENT: Reflect on the moment you became saved. Challenge yourself to bless others with that same life changing experience. Write a proclamation declaring your commitment to winning souls to the kingdom.

Thoughts of today's journey....

_____

_____

_____

_____

_____

_____

_____

_____

_____

_____

_____

DAY Twelve ~ Preparation

❖ Before I formed thee in the belly I knew thee; and before thou camest forth out of the womb I sanctified thee, and I ordained thee a prophet unto the nations. Jeremiah 1:5

Dear Lord,

Thank You for preparing me for the things my eyes have not seen, my ears have not heard, my mind has not conceived, nor my heart imagined. I rejoice, because my future is in Your hands and through your Holy Spirit I am able to conceptualize so many possibilities.

I acknowledge that I need You by my side. I strive to live the life You have predestined for me. Remove any blinders that may be restricting my vision and eliminate distractions that may be hindering my progress. Separate me from those who are strategically placed to delay my promises and suffocate my potential. I ask that You would strategically bless me with relationships that will lift me, encourage me and push me to fulfill every assignment on my life.

Thank You in advance for preparing me. AMEN

TODAY'S ASSIGNMENT: Consider life as it stands today? List any necessary changes that must take place in order to move to the next tier in your spiritual life. Is there anything restricting your growth? Relationships? Attitudes? Behaviors? Contemplate these things and invite God to begin the process of adjusting these areas.

Thoughts of today's journey....

_____

_____

_____

_____

_____

_____

_____

_____

_____

_____

_____

DAY Thirteen ~ Excuses

❖ Now therefore go, and I will be with thy mouth, and teach thee what thou shalt say.
Exodus 4: 12

Dear Lord,

Clearly, You don't need permission to use my life. You created me on purpose with purpose and I honor You for allowing me an opportunity to serve in Your Kingdom. Help me Lord to be grateful that I have been chosen and allow me to see the blessing in being selected to work for You. Help me not to be so focused on my selfish desires that I fail to be responsive and serious about this calling upon my life. Purge me from the tendency to complain, conjure excuses, or drag my feet, when You have need of me. Keep in the forefront of my mind that others are dependent upon my obedience and that Your will is all that matters.

I thank You Lord, for walking with me, lessening my anxiety and easing my mind as You call me into uncharted territory. Forgive me from poor attempts to justify my reservations, especially when You have never failed me or led me astray.

Bless me to walk without fear and reservation and with a spirit of confidence and pride and commitment to Your way.   AMEN

TODAY'S ASSIGNMENT: Compose a list of frequently used excuses with God. Make a verbal and written commitment to refrain from using them.

Thoughts of today's journey....

_____

_____

_____

_____

_____

_____

_____

_____

_____

_____

DAY Fourteen ~ Stillness

❖ "Be still, and know that I am God. " Psalm 46:10

Dear Lord,

Teach me how to quiet my thoughts and sit still in Your presence that I may hear You speak. Calm my hectic world and impart into me the beauty that is to be found, while sitting free from distractions before You. I admit that many days I lack the discipline necessary to simply be still. Bless me Lord with much needed self control, that I may enter into deeper places in You.

As You speak Lord, I will listen. AMEN

TODAY'S ASSIGNMENT: Sit for a minimum of 30 minutes in the still quiet presence of God. Record your experience.

Thoughts of today's journey....

_____

_____

_____

_____

_____

_____

_____

_____

_____

_____

DAY Fifteen ~ Blessing

❖ And Jabez called on the God of Israel, saying, Oh
that thou wouldest bless me indeed, and enlarge
my coast, and that thine hand might be with me,
and that thou wouldest keep me from evil, that it
may not grieve me! And God granted him that
which he requested. 1 Chronicles 4: 10

Dear Lord,

You are a great and awesome God! Thank You
for another day to share in such a meaningful
relationship that is growing deeper and more
beautiful by the day. I exalt You for ALL that
You are and I appreciate this closeness that is
fully mine to enjoy.

Today, I ask just as You blessed Jabez that You
would also bless me indeed. I am in position for
you to bless me however it pleases You. I ask
BOLDLY for every perfect blessing You have
divinely designed specifically for me. I thank
You for I am confident in my spirit that they are
in direct route.

Thank You for every blessing that will
contribute to my emotional healing. Thank You
for every blessing that will contribute to my
physical healing. Thank You for every blessing
that will contribute to my mental healing.

Thank you for every blessing that will contribute to my spiritual healing. Thank You for every blessing that will establish my financial security.

Thank You for every unique life experience that is shaping such an amazing testimony that glorifies You and speaks to Your ability and might! I praise You, because You alone are worthy. I adore You and esteem You above all others. Thank You for being my God, and for every rich blessing over my life!!!
AMEN!

TODAY'S ASSIGNMENT: Dare to ask God today for EVERY blessing He desires you to have.

Thoughts of today's journey....

_____

_____

_____

_____

_____

_____

_____

_____

_____

_____

_____

DAY Sixteen ~ Connection

❖ Hear counsel, and receive instruction, that thou mayest be wise in thy latter end. Proverbs 19:20

Dear Lord,

How EXCELLENT is Your name! You are greatly to be praised and I consider it a privilege to be in intimate fellowship with You.

I am sincerely grateful for Your omniscience in assigning people to my life to impart wisdom and provide godly counsel. Give me an open and willing spirit to receive the guidance and correction that is lovingly given. Continue to increase my network with those who are kingdom and mission-minded.

Increase my discernment to recognize, when relationships are in direct conflict with Your divine plan for me and my household. I pray that You would expose relationships that have served their purpose and run their course. Bless me with courage and conviction to separate myself from what has come to an end and prepare me to move forward toward the next phase of life that awaits.

Thank You Lord for constructing my life and relationships in a manor that blesses me and is pleasing to You. AMEN!

TODAY'S ASSIGNMENT: Evaluate the influences in your life. Seek God's direction on your present relationships. Be in prayerful consideration, while making necessary adjustments.

Thoughts of today's journey....

_____

_____

_____

_____

_____

_____

_____

_____

_____

_____

_____

_____

Day Seventeen ~ Worth

❖ **Jesus and the woman of Samaria. John 4: 1-29**

Dear Lord,

I am overwhelmed at the thought of knowing that regardless of how I may have strayed Your love has never given up on me. Words are inadequate, when thinking of the danger You lovingly carried me through. Without a second thought, You rescue me over and over again. My heart fills with reverence to know that Your plans for my life were not compromised by my foolish decisions. Thank You for saving me, when I was drowning in a life of sin and shame. I am so amazed that You care so much for me. It is truly a wonder that You would dare bless me with a life full of promise and great reward.

Because You would not let me go, I now know what true love is. I am driven to worship You, because without cause You love me. Because You cherish me, unconditional grace and mercy has found its way to me.

Thank You for looking beyond my faults and seeing just how much I need Savior. AMEN

TODAY'S ASSIGNMENT: Recall the many experiences when God reached past your present predicament in order to rescue you. Write a thank you letter expressing your gratitude.

Thoughts of today's journey....

_____

_____

_____

_____

_____

_____

_____

_____

_____

_____

_____

Day Eighteen ~ Compassion

❖ Now the God of patience and consolation grant
you to be likeminded one toward another
according to Christ Jesus: That ye may with one
mind and one mouth glorify God, even the Father
of our Lord Jesus Christ. Wherefore receive ye
one another, as Christ also received us to the
glory of God. Romans 15: 5-7

Dear Lord,

Your patient kindness is never failing. I
welcome Your guidance as You teach, edify and
correct me. I pray that just as You have been
faithful in walking with me, that I too will have a
level of sensitivity as I am used to share the
Gospel with others. Keep me aware of my
personal development process, so that I am
never judgmental concerning the struggles
involved when one makes a life changing
decision follow You.

My desire is to continue being faithful,
trustworthy, and vigilant in Your Kingdom, and
with divine assistance I know I can and will
remain focused and useful. AMEN

TODAY'S ASSIGNMENT: Ponder over the area of service God has called you to. Seek The Lord's blessings upon your service. Write a list of your strengths in God's service. With a thankful heart meditate on the awesome opportunities God has given you to serve Him.

Thoughts of today's journey....

_____

_____

_____

_____

_____

_____

_____

_____

_____

_____

_____

Day Nineteen ~ Difficult Seasons

❖ **The Lord shall fight for you, and ye shall hold your peace. Exodus 14: 14**

Dear Lord,

As I reflect over challenges in my life, I am confident that EVERYTHING taking place is contributing to my development. I'm noticing how my faith increases, while I'm being navigated through undesirable life lessons. Your word secures, encourages, gives me hope; and I am certain that I would be lost without it!

I realize Your strength is what holds back the enemy who actively seeks to destroy my relationships, health, faith, finances and future. How can I ever thank You for the divine protection that covers me and the peace in knowing that my God is always fighting for me.

I praise You for sustaining power in uncomfortable, difficult seasons that craft my unique testimony for Your glory. I am clear, that no storm lasts forever, and that all things will work together to showcase just how AWESOME my God is! AMEN

TODAY'S ASSIGNMENT: Take the time to begin writing/ recording your personal testimony.

Thoughts of today's journey....

_____

_____

_____

_____

_____

_____

_____

_____

_____

_____

_____

_____

Day Twenty ~ Restoration

❖ **And when He had sent the multitudes away, He went up into a mountain apart to pray: and when the evening was come, He was there alone. Matthew 14: 22**

Dear Lord,

You know all too well that although I am called to Your service, I live a normal life, packed with very real, emotional experiences. I appreciate Your word that offers instruction and guidance to ensure a successful, positive and productive life.

I recognize, that if I am ever going to maximize my potential, I must live by Christ's example in being sensitive to my physical and emotional needs. I pray for increased discipline, as I develop in ministry. Speak to me during times, when I must pull away from my work in order for You to breathe on me, restoring and replenishing my mind, body and spirit.

Keep me in tune with my human limitations and deliver me from the tendency to say "yes" when a "no" is in order. I pray that I become obedient to the unction of the Holy Spirit, when I'm being instructed to withdraw. I understand that when I am at my personal best, I am a better representation of You.

Thank You Lord for Your restoring power. I receive it in Jesus' name. AMEN

TODAY'S ASSIGNMENT: Schedule a regular personal retreat with God. Review your calendar and set aside time for renewal monthly, whether it's one day, half-day, or a few hours

Thoughts of today's journey….

_____

_____

_____

_____

_____

_____

_____

_____

_____

_____

_____

Day Twenty-one ~ Manifestation

❖ And Jacob was left alone; and there wrestled a man with him until the breaking of the day. And when he saw that he prevailed not against him, he touched the hollow of his thigh; and the hollow of Jacob's thigh was out of joint, as he wrestled with him. And he said, Let me go, for the day breaketh. And he said, I will not let thee go, except thou bless me. **Genesis 32: 24-26**

Dear Lord,

What must I do to bring forth promises and power in my life? I need a blessing from You and I'm willing to do what it takes to receive it. I will be brave, regardless of what comes before me. I will be strong. I will not waver. I will be courageous. I will not turn back. I will not give up. I will not doubt. I will not fear. I will not question Your will for my life. I will not let go, until You bless me.

I need You to show up and be MIGHTY! I need Your help! My hope is in You. My faith is in You. I am expecting YOU TO MANIFEST Your absolute power and presence in my life! I will not let go, until You bless me. AMEN

TODAY'S ASSIGNMENT: Pay attention to how God moves for you today. Write everything you notice... no matter how large or small.

Thoughts of today's journey....

_____

_____

_____

_____

_____

_____

_____

_____

_____

_____

_____

_____

_____

_____

_____

_____

DAY Twenty-two ~ Gratitude

❖ Trust in the Lord, and do good; so shalt thou dwell in the land, and verily thou shalt be fed. Delight thyself also in the Lord; and He shall give thee the desires of thine heart. Commit thy way unto the Lord; trust also in Him; and He shall bring it to pass. Psalm 37: 3-5

Dear Lord,

Your loving kindness toward me grants so many opportunities and blessings that I have not earned, and do not deserve... I recognize Your hand moving in my life daily, and I am eternally grateful.

If I had ten thousand tongues, I could never praise You enough for all of Your unbelievable goodness toward me. With a joyful heart I celebrate Your generosity that blesses me beyond measure, and I excitedly await the many promises that are soon to come to pass.

I clearly understand that Your mercy is what allows me to benefit from Your endless bounty. I pray that You continue to position me to bless others as You have freely given unto me. AMEN

TODAY'S ASSIGNMENT: Put in writing every promise you can remember God giving you. Thank Him in advance, in writing, for what is about to come to pass.

Thoughts of today's journey....

_____

_____

_____

_____

_____

_____

_____

_____

_____

_____

_____

Day Twenty-three ~ Wisdom

❖ **If any of you lack wisdom, let him ask of God, that giveth to all men liberally, and upbraideth not; and it shall be given him. But let him ask in faith, nothing wavering. James 1:5**

Dear Lord,

I desire to see situations, as You see them and respond accordingly with spiritual principles. I ask that You would impart unto me what is to be learned in Your word and motivate me to seek, meditate, obey and apply the scriptures, that are intended to build and shape my character.

Please grant me wisdom to quickly discern, make sound decisions in critical moments and to know, when I may be drifting from your plans concerning me. I know that without wisdom I am unable to distinguish the difference between truth and deception, therefore I seek wisdom and clarity for it positions me to live a blessed life that serves me well and benefits others around me.

Overshadow my thought process and infuse me with Your Holy Spirit, as I live from day to day. I thank You in advance for the spiritual and mental edification, that is required to excel in the areas I am called to serve.

I give You thanks for the daily renewing of my mind that enables me to grow in Godly wisdom and for blessing me with those placed in my life, to offer enlightenment throughout my journey. AMEN

TODAY'S ASSIGNMENT: Ask God to increase your wisdom and understanding through a written prayer. Note any new revelations you experience over the remainder of this 30 day journey.

Thoughts of today's journey....

Day Twenty-four ~ Contentment

❖ I know both how to be abased, and I know how to abound: everywhere and in all things I am instructed both to be full and to be hungry, both to abound and to suffer need. I can do all things through Christ which strengtheneth me. Philippians 4:12

Dear Lord,

Lord I trust You! I vow to keep You as the center of my life. I praise You for the peace that passes all understanding, because is only through You that I am not consumed by daily issues that pull at me and test my faith. I am certain, that whether I am in a season of lack or a season of plenty, YOU are always in control. Therefore, I will rest in Your comfort.

Your promise to never leave me alone gives me the strength I need to overcome, whatever challenge or changes I must endure. I am absolutely confident that You love me and that Your desire for my life is to be victorious, in all things.

Thank You for being the anchor that secures my spirit and guarantees my outcome! AMEN

TODAY'S ASSIGNMENT: Acknowledge The Lord for sustaining you regardless of the season at hand. Honor the Lord today by speaking life into someone who needs to be uplifted.

Thoughts of today's journey....

Day Twenty-five ~ Go

❖ **Therefore now go, lead the people unto the place of which I have spoken unto thee Exodus 32: 34**

Dear Lord,

You alone are my Guide. Grant me a willing, obedient spirit to quickly go where I am, without hesitation. Help me to understand that there are repercussions, when I allow trepidation to frighten and hinder me. I pray to be kept from making costly mistakes that jeopardize my future, as well as the future of those depending me.

When I feel weak and uncertain, bring to my remembrance the fact that there is no weapon formed against me that will be able to ever prosper. Also, remind me that You have always made provision for your children, who were sent on assignment.

I thank you God, for choosing, equipping, directing and protecting me, on the path You have predetermined for me. AMEN

TODAY'S ASSIGNMENT: Take notice of the unnecessary, costly detours experienced, in your life. Have a heartfelt conversation with God regarding your realizations. Make a conscious effort to walk daily in obedience to the Holy Spirit. Open your mind and spirit to the direction of the Holy Spirit.

Thoughts of today's journey….

_____

_____

_____

_____

_____

_____

_____

_____

_____

_____

Day Twenty-six ~ Serve

❖ Not with eye service, as men-pleasers; but as the servants of Christ, doing the will of God from the heart; With good will doing service, as to the Lord, and not to men: Knowing that whatsoever good thing any man doeth, the same shall he receive of the Lord, whether he be bond or free. Ephesians 6: 6-8

Dear Lord,

I love and adore You. It is my esteemed privilege to serve You, with all that I am.

As I wake daily, my desire is to walk worthy, never losing sight of why I live and whom I am living for. Bless me with a continual awareness of You and a humbleness that makes surrendering to Your will easy.

Hide Your word in my heart and keep me sensitive of Your thoughts toward me. I am thankful for the opportunity to serve You, by serving those You place in my path. Identify the works my hands have been anointed to complete and give me a determination to finish every task, with a mindset of dedication and excellence.

Help me Lord to manage my gifts and keep me from mundane tasks that waste precious time. I acknowledge the privilege to represent Your love and compassion and I praise You for the great reward that will be mine, when I am living eternally with You. AMEN.

TODAY'S ASSIGNMENT: Determine in what capacity you find joy as you invest your time and talent. Commit or recommit yourself to service in God's Kingdom, with your time and talents. Consider mentorship, if you are one who is regularly involved in a ministry of service.

Thoughts of today's journey....

_____

_____

_____

_____

_____

_____

_____

_____

_____

_____

_____

_____

Day Twenty-seven ~ Test

And Moses said unto the people, Fear not: for God is come to prove you, and that his fear may be before your faces, that ye sin not. And the people stood afar off, and Moses drew near unto the thick darkness where God was. Exodus 20: 20

Dear Lord,

It is my pleasure to praise and worship You, for You alone are my strength and shield. Where would I be without You? What would life be without You? My test would defeat me, if it were not for You.

I stand in awe of how You reveal yourself to me, especially in the midst of life's tests. I am aware that I was never promised a life without hardship, therefore I am appreciative that You have never left me alone in my seasons of testing. Instead, You stand with me in the fire, molding me and perfecting me for my divine purpose.

I am grateful that you take the necessary time to shape me, in moments of testing. I see now that my tests are making me stronger and developing my character. Because of your commitment to me, I am forever inspired to live a lifestyle of pure worship.

I love You Lord.... even in the midst of the difficult tests. I know they have purpose. AMEN.

TODAY'S ASSIGNMENT: Rest in your test. Know that God is with you. Look and identify signs of His presence.

Thoughts of today's journey....

_____

_____

_____

_____

_____

_____

_____

_____

_____

_____

_____

Day Twenty-eight ~ Grace

❖ **But the God of all grace, who hath called us unto his eternal glory by Christ Jesus, after that ye have suffered a while, make you perfect, stablish, strengthen, settle you. 1 Peter 5:10**

Dear Lord,

I could never repay You, for the unmerited favor I receive freely from day to day. I clearly recall so many instances that should have discounted me from Your grace, but Your boundless love refuses to turn away from me.

I am humbled that You choose to love someone like me so much and find use for me in Your Kingdom.

Thank You Lord. I am forever grateful. Forever changed. Forever committed to You. AMEN

TODAY'S ASSIGNMENT: Search your heart. Determine if there is anyone in your life that requires your grace and forgiveness. Seek God for the strength to extend grace and forgiveness, in order to move to the next place in your spiritual journey.

Thoughts of today's journey....

_____

_____

_____

_____

_____

_____

_____

_____

_____

_____

_____

_____

Day Twenty-nine ~ Willing

❖ But be ye doers of the word, and not hearers only, deceiving your own selves.   James 1: 22

Dear Lord,

I acknowledge You as and Lord and Savior, in my life. I am so blessed to experience a genuine evolving relationship with You, the GREAT and LIVING God.

Thank You for speaking in a language I understand and being patient with me, as I am being conditioned to hear and recognize Your voice. I pray for an anointing to consistently HEAR clearly, as I continue this journey of knowing You and all understanding who You are. Lord, I don't want to be confused, distracted nor afraid.

Father, I fully embrace Your word and am prepared and willing to carry it out. Grant me the confidence, power and strength to overcome fear, break yokes and walk in confidence. I desire so deeply to be used by You and yield results that increase Your Kingdom.

I renounce my former self and give You complete control, in this new walk that is sure to be life-changing.

Grant me an undying tenacity to consistently search after You, that I may develop into a perfect and beautiful likeness of You.

Lord I love you... completely... with my whole heart. I give myself away. AMEN

TODAY'S ASSIGNMENT: Sit quietly today in God's presence for 30 minutes twice today and record your experience.

Thoughts of today's journey....

_____

_____

_____

_____

_____

_____

_____

_____

_____

_____

_____

_____

Day Thirty ~ Love

❖ So when they had rowed about five and twenty or thirty furlongs, they see Jesus walking on the sea, and drawing nigh unto the ship: and they were afraid. But he saith unto them, "it is I; be not afraid." Then they willingly received him into the ship: and immediately the ship was at the land whither they went John 6: 19-21

Sovereign Lord,

I thank You for loving me enough to prove yourself. Thank You for transforming our relationship into something that is real, special, unique and indescribable. You are amazing and words fail to encompass all of who You are.

I am thankful for what is just the beginning of a life-long journey we will take together. I am humbled that You would take the time to walk with, talk to and teach me. My eyes are now opening to how You constantly shower me with your presence and how readily available Your word and Your Spirit is to me. Like a deer, I find myself panting for the deeper things in You. I thirst for Your voice to rise in my spirit.

God, I am officially Yours! I vow to live for You. I vow to breathe for You. I vow to sing for You. I vow to minister for You. I vow to give for You. My desire is to bring You glory, in all I do.

Thank you for allowing me to be your child and considering me worthy enough to experience Your presence. A life with and in you excites me and causes my heart to soar. A life apart from You is no longer an option! I will not turn back. I will continue walking forward focused on the path you have laid before me. Thank You Father.... for choosing me.

AMEN

TODAY'S ASSIGNMENT: Move forward in expectancy of a life FULL of God's power and presence. DO NOT TURN BACK!!!!!

Thoughts of My Journey....

_____

_____

_____

_____

_____

_____

_____

_____

_____

_____

_____

_____

About the author:

Rev. Tameaka Reid Sims, is recognized as a vibrant, powerful and anointed preacher, teacher and role model. She is passionate about prayer, evangelism, and outreach; and is especially gifted to minister to the needs of women through a national women's ministry. Rev. Sims is the founder of Tameaka Reid Sims Ministries, Executive Pastor of Bethel A.M.E. Church in Harrisburg, Pa, the loving wife of Rev. Micah C.T. Sims, and the extremely proud mother of 5.

For more information on Tameaka Reid Sims log onto www.TameakaReidSims.com

Made in the USA
Lexington, KY
24 December 2017